Contents

1 The rise of the East India Company

In 1600 Queen Elizabeth I of England granted a charter to a company of merchants in London trading with the East Indies. This was done 'as well for the honour of this our realm of England as for the increase of our navigation and advancement of trade and merchandise'. So from the start the English government was involved in the affairs of the East India Company, and there was nothing strange in this. At that time Portugal claimed to be the only European nation entitled to trade in the eastern seas. Portugal was ruled by the King of Spain, and England was at war with Spain. So, by breaking Portugal's monopoly, the merchants of the Company would be fighting the Queen's battles.

The Portuguese were not the only reason why the English merchants needed to have both guns and official backing. There was always the danger of pirates, of course. Eastern rulers might suspect the merchants themselves of being pirates unless they could show that they had the approval of their own kings. Perhaps the greatest danger at this time, however, was the competition of other European merchants who would not hesitate to use force if they thought it would succeed. Indeed, the Dutch soon drove the English out of the East Indies islands, so that the English had to concentrate on trading in the subcontinent of India.

In these circumstances the merchants needed to have trading posts, or factories as they were called, which they could fortify and defend. For this, they had to obtain

above: *A Portuguese picture of Surat, 1614. Soldiers and war-galleys defend the settlement, and walled commercial area across the river, from an attack.*

left: *The merchants of the East India Company met in different houses in London until 1648, when they moved into this house in Leadenhall Street. (Print copied from a Dutch painting.)*

permission from the ruler of the country. In seventeenth-century India, this would usually mean the Mogul Emperor. The English were not the only ones who sought and obtained such posts, as the map shows. The Dutch were there, but they were more interested in the East Indies and Ceylon. Portugal was weakening, and needed English help when she rose and fought for her independence against Spain. So it happened that by the early eighteenth century the French Company was the main rival of the English. At this time, too, England and France were often opposed to each other in European wars and politics.

Just at the time when Anglo-French rivalry was growing the strength of the Mogul Emperors was collapsing. This meant that other princes, some of them supposed to be no more than governors appointed by the Emperor, seized control over more and more kingdoms and provinces. Even at the height of Mogul power, the Emperor had never ruled the whole subcontinent and had never been free from war with neighbouring rulers and revolts among his subjects; for India was not one country, one nation, but many.

The English and French recognized the dangers, and strengthened their defences. They raised regiments of Indian soldiers trained to fight in the European way, besides bringing in European troops and, when war broke out, asking for the help of government troops and ships. They also saw that there were new opportunities as well as new dangers. They could try to influence, perhaps even control, a local ruler so that he would favour them and make things awkward for their rivals.

The French and English fought it out in the mid-century wars which were known in Europe as the War of the Austrian Succession and the Seven Years War. The English won. Though the French still retained factories in India, and for many years there were Frenchmen with ideas of reversing the English victory, the fact was that after 1763 the English East India Company was too powerful to be overthrown by anything the French could do. The English Company – or rather the British, after the Union of the English and Scottish Parliaments in 1707 – had itself become the ruler of vast and rich kingdoms in India.

This result had not been intended or foreseen. The really decisive development came when the British became involved in war with the ruler of Bengal and, after defeating

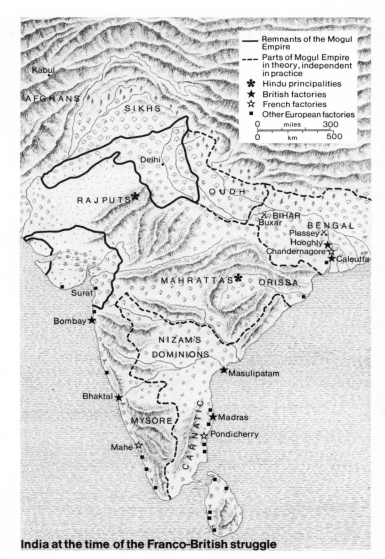

India at the time of the Franco-British struggle

him at Plassey in 1757, set up another in his place. From this moment the British held the real power in Bengal, and soon began to enjoy it. Their puppets tried to challenge them, but the British put them down, and in 1765 the Mogul officially recognized the Company as ruler of Bengal, Bihar and Orissa. In Orissa the Mahrattas stayed on in occupation, but the official authority was nevertheless the Company.

5

2 Government and conquest

In the 1760s there were three main centres of British power in India; Bombay, Madras and Calcutta. The territory which was ruled from each city became known as a Presidency, and each had its own Governor. But they were not equal, for the Bengal Presidency was far bigger and richer than the others. The first Governor of Bengal was the victor of Plassey, Robert Clive. Though from 1765 the Company held power officially, the British still found it useful to keep up the fiction that the Indian Nawab, or ruler, still reigned, and the existing system of government continued. The differ-ence was that the British demanded money and were quite ready to interfere if they did not get what they wanted, so the old system of government, which had been in a bad state before the British arrived, became little better than chaos.

In this chaos the strong and crafty, both Indian and British, enriched themselves through taxes, trading privi-leges, loans, rents and bribes. The weak were squeezed harder and harder for money. Lord Clive himself wrote that Calcutta was one of the wickedest places in the world: 'Corruption, Licentiousness & a want of Principle seem to

Fort St George. An engraving published in 1794. The English were granted a strip of land on the south-east coast of India in 1639 by the Hindu Raja of Chandagiri. They were also given permission to build this fort there to protect themselves and their merchandise. In time it grew into the great city of Madras.

have possess'd the minds of all the Civil Servants, by frequent bad Examples they have grown callous, Rapacious & Luxurious beyond Conception.'

Clive himself was less than perfect, though, and when he returned to Britain he was accused of oppression and corruption and had to submit to a Parliamentary inquiry. The business depressed him so badly that eventually he killed himself.

Clive's tragedy had one good side. Parliament in Britain was beginning to realize that it had to accept a share of the responsibility – and power – which the Company had assumed in India. The first Act of Parliament to legislate for India was passed in 1773. The Company was badly in debt, and had asked Parliament for help. Parliament decided that it must make sure that there was better supervision of what was going on. In India the Governor of Bengal became Governor-General, superior to the Governors of Madras and Bombay. In England the Directors of the Company had to show their letters and accounts to Parliament. This was called the Regulating Act, but it did not make at all clear what would happen if the British government disagreed with what the Directors in London or the Governor-General in Calcutta was doing.

The Act also set up a Supreme Court in Calcutta. This was well meant, for justice was sorely needed. But it marks the beginning of a long series of attempts to impose on India

The Mogul Emperor, Shah Alam, granting to Clive in 1765 the right to control Bengal. The painting is by Benjamin West who, though not present, was an artist who usually tried to bring out the historical importance of such series.

The British Resident at the Mogul court of Delhi riding in a state procession of the Emperor Akbar II in about 1815. The Resident sits in a howdah on the first elephant.

the laws and ideas of the British. These may or may not have been better than Indian ways, but what is certain is that they were often misunderstood and resented by many Indians.

The first Governor-General was Warren Hastings. He seriously wanted to improve the government of the millions of Indians placed under his authority, but he respected and liked Indians and their civilization. Hastings however made many enemies, both British and Indian, and when he returned to Britain was, like Clive, attacked in Parliament for what his enemies alleged to be his greedy and tyrannical behaviour. Hastings was acquitted at the end of a long and complicated trial, and, though historians still argue about him, this was probably a good verdict. It seems that the people who had found Hastings a harsh ruler were the rich and powerful, and that he had tried to make life a little less hard and unfair for the ordinary Indians.

Meanwhile another Regulating Act was passed, in 1784, to clarify and strengthen what had been left vague in the previous Act. In London, Parliament set up a Board of Control to supervise the Directors of the Company, and

ordered that the Chairman of the Directors should act only in close consultation with the President of the Board. In India, the powers of the Governor-General were increased. So Parliament, through the Board and the Directors, could give orders to a Governor-General who was now made strong enough to rule unchallenged in the British parts of India.

But it could take as long as six months for letters and instructions to pass between London and Calcutta. Therefore Parliamentary control over the Company's officials in India was a slow and complicated business. It was inevitable that they would often act first and consult London later. This was the origin of a system of dual control over the affairs of British India, legally by Parliament but effectively by the Company's men. It lasted for seventy years and gave power in India to a number of able governors and officials.

These men were like Warren Hastings in wanting to rule well, and in not being afraid to use their authority vigorously. Unlike Hastings, though, they tended to assume that British civilization was in every way superior to Indian. The

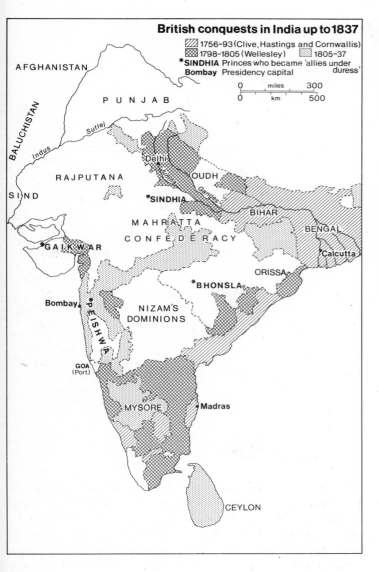

British conquests in India up to 1837

- ▨ 1756–93 (Clive, Hastings and Cornwallis)
- ▩ 1798–1805 (Wellesley)
- ▦ 1805–37
- *SINDHIA Princes who became 'allies under duress'
- Bombay Presidency capital

miles 0 — 300
km 0 — 500

AFGHANISTAN

BALUCHISTAN

PUNJAB

Indus *Sutlej*

RAJPUTANA

SIND

Delhi

OUDH

Jumna *Ganges*

*SINDHIA

BIHAR

MAHRATTA
CONFEDERACY

BENGAL

*GAIKWAR

Calcutta

ORISSA

*BHONSLA

Bombay

NIZAM'S
DOMINIONS

*PEISHWA

GOA
(Port.)

MYSORE

Madras

CEYLON

---

not share power with Indians, and gradually came to regard themselves as a race of rulers, quite separate from the people they ruled. India had been invaded many times over the centuries, but all the earlier invaders had settled down in the subcontinent, intermarried with the peoples they had overcome and, despite even deep religious differences, had become Indians. The British were different.

British feelings of superiority were nourished by a succession of victorious wars that made the Company ruler of the greater part of India. The map shows the way their empire grew. No earlier conqueror in the subcontinent could match these successes. Despite one or two failures, the worst being the disastrous retreat from Kabul in Afghanistan in 1842, the progress of British power seemed irresistible. Many of the British now saw themselves as 'Romans among Barbarians', carrying out their civilizing mission without much regard for the feelings of the Indians, who must learn to accept the better things that their masters were bringing them.

By Queen Victoria's reign the East India Company had really ceased to be a commercial concern and it was no longer making assured profits. It had become the field of activity of men who wished to see the creation of a strong empire that would display Britain's power in the world. Britain was becoming an industrialized country, ever more dependent on trade and manufacture. India with her vast population supplying raw materials to Britain and purchasing finished goods was to be the power base of this empire.

Does all this mean that the Company or the British government deliberately set about conquering India for their own selfish reasons? Probably not, especially at first. Wars had always been common in India, and naturally when the British became important rulers they were drawn into the alliances and enmities of the Indian states. But the British nearly always won, and held firmly what they took. As their territories grew, it is likely that many of their most energetic and ambitious men came to look forward to spreading an empire over the whole subcontinent, partly for their own profit and glory and partly for the good of the Indians. However the motives may have been mixed at different times and with different people, one thing was certain. Force was going to be needed, and the Company's main weapon of war was its sepoy army.

most important posts in all branches of the administration of British India were reserved for British men. One reason for this was to attract really good officials instead of the very mixed collection who had so often proved corrupt and lazy in the past, and on the whole the idea succeeded. The new officials were much more efficient and honest. But they did

3 The Company's army

The sepoys

Units of Indian sepoys (from the Hindustani word *sipahi*, a soldier) were first raised by the East India Company in Bombay, then in Madras, and finally in Bengal. The armies of the three Presidencies developed separately according to the special needs of each area of India. Eventually the Bengal army, first raised by Clive in 1757, became the most numerous and powerful. This was because the task it was given was nothing less than the conquest of the whole of north India.

Although the nucleus of the Company's army in the early nineteenth century continued to be British regiments specially enlisted for service in India, and although regiments of the regular British army were stationed in India, there were seldom as many as 40,000 British soldiers in the whole subcontinent. Rather it was an army of 200,000 Indian troops who brought India under the control of the British Company.

The military mutiny which started the great Rebellion of 1857 took place only in the Bengal army, and we must examine the nature and origins of this army and its grievances to find out why the mutiny happened.

When Clive started to recruit Indians he did not enlist Bengalis, for they were not considered to be a martial people. He enlisted instead soldiers of fortune, mercenaries from all over the Mogul Empire. They were fierce military adventurers from Bihar, Oudh, Afghanistan and Rajasthan. Among them were men of many different nations and faiths, Jats, Pathans, Rajputs, some Hindu and some Muslim. Men of the highest social classes became soldiers because, in India, after teaching religion, bearing arms was the most honourable profession.

The sepoys were given the same sort of uniforms and weapons as the British and were drilled in the same tactics

A sepoy of the 21st Battalion, Bengal Native Infantry, at the beginning of the nineteenth century. He is a grenadier, that is a soldier especially chosen for size and strength. This is shown on his cap badge. The mark on his forehead means he is an Indian of high caste, probably a Brahmin.

and disciplines of war. As the risks of the Company's involvement in Bengal increased, so Clive raised more regiments. Soon there were five, each of 1,000 sepoys, commanded by British officers, trained by British sergeants and having also their own Indian officers and non-commissioned officers. This raising of regiments did not please the Directors of the Company in London, however, because it was an expensive business and they were interested in the pursuit of profits. Nevertheless the need to protect British property and to threaten force while collecting taxes caused Clive to increase still further the size of the Bengal army.

In August 1765 he divided it into three brigades. Each

The Company's Bengal army, 1757-1857

In 1757 the Bengal army consisted of a few hundred British, recruited in Britain by the Company.

Clive added companies of sepoys, each with a British officer in command and a British sergeant. These were later formed into sepoy regiments.

After 1758 five regiments were organized, and within a few years there were many more, grouped in brigades with the Company's British units.

A **sepoy regiment** consisted of:

Regimental H.Q.:
- British commanding officer
- Senior Indian officer
- British special officers (e.g.surgeon)
- British senior N.C.O.

<u>Note</u> Exact numbers of British would vary according to local custom, availability and quality of Indian officers.

5 companies commanded by:
- British officer
- Indian officer
- British N.C.O.

4 platoons of 50 sepoys in each company commanded by 1 senior and 4 other Indian N.C.O.s

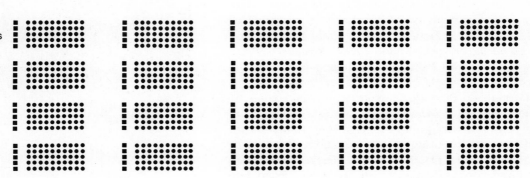

A **brigade** consisted of:

7 regiments of infantry

British   Indian

1 troop of cavalry

 Indian cavalry regiments were added later.

1 company of artillery

 Occasionally the gunners were Indian.

The Bengal army after 1765 consisted of 3 brigades.

Though uniforms changed and the size of the armies varied from time to time, this pattern of organization was basically still the rule in 1857.

brigade consisted of six sepoy regiments, one British infantry regiment, a troop of cavalry and a company of artillery. These brigades were self-contained, independent forces and were stationed in important strategic places where they could threaten the enemies of the Company and encourage its allies. Clive saw the necessity of having equal numbers of Hindus and Muslims in his brigades. These were placed in different companies, not only to encourage competition in military qualities, but also to lessen the chances of their combining together against their officers.

The Company's wars in the late eighteenth century were not confined to the north of India. The conflicts with Mysore and with the Mahrattas involved the armies of the Madras and Bombay Presidencies. However, it was easier to recruit sepoys among the traditionally warrior peoples of the north than in any other part of India, and by 1780 the Bengal army had grown to thirty-five regiments.

At this time sepoys received 6 rupees per month, *naiks* (corporals) 8 and *havildars* (sergeants) 16. The senior Indian officer of each regiment, called the *subadar*, received 60 rupees. In addition all ranks received about half of these amounts as *batta*, or special allowances. A rupee in those days was equivalent to 2 shillings of English money of the same period, but it would buy much more than 2 shillings would in England. Pay was augmented on campaign by prize money and there were opportunities for loot also. Half-way pensions were paid to long-serving soldiers after at least fifteen years' continuous service, and land grants, or *jagirs*, could be taken instead of cash. These grants were made of jungle or wasteland which could be turned into prosperous holdings. A *subadar* would receive about 200 acres, a *havildar* 60 and a sepoy 40. For most of those who enlisted, however, the principal motive was not financial gain or to receive a grant of land. They were already men of substance in their villages. The main reason was the respect they enjoyed in their military profession and the support they received from the Company's officials if they ever had a dispute about landholdings in their villages.

The sepoys, then, were proud men from the higher classes. They had their servants on campaign and were looked up to by their own people. To encourage regimental pride they were given smart and distinctive uniforms: in about 1800, a short, brightly coloured jacket, a white shirt,

A later print of sepoys: different members of the 21st Madras Native Infantry in the middle of the nineteenth century.

white breeches halfway down the thigh and a splendid tall head-dress. They carried their bayonets like daggers in a wide sash of the regimental colour. On many occasions they gave evidence of their courage, toughness and patience under the most difficult conditions of war far from their own

The Indian sepoys fought in difficult faraway places to establish British power in India. This sketch shows a mountain pass in Baluchistan in the north-western regions. Some tribesmen are waiting in ambush, but above them the sepoy picket is preparing a surprise attack. From Sketches in Afghanistan *by J. Atkinson, 1842.*

homes and villages. They showed a fierce loyalty to the British officers who commanded them.

However, as the Company's dominions became more widespread and the numbers of sepoys increased, so the opportunities for grievances and misunderstandings became more numerous.

Grievances of the sepoys

In 1782 and 1795 some regiments which had refused to be transported by sea were disbanded. This refusal was reasonable because on their enlistment the sepoys had not contracted to serve overseas. To leave the soil of India, moreover, would cause the Hindu sepoy to become an outcast because his religion and custom forbade it.

In 1824 a serious mutiny occurred among sepoy regiments which were to have been sent by sea to Rangoon in Burma, but by now this was not the sole reason for trouble. There was also a growing lack of leadership and understanding on the part of the British officers. Many of these officers had

become too old and unfit for service, and others had come to India only to make money and had no interest in their men. Pay had not kept up with the cost of living and the sepoy was expected to house, feed and equip himself from his small salary.

In 1842 a war in Afghanistan, incompetently managed, resulted in a disastrous retreat from Kabul. The Company's forces were harried into a rout and the entire army of 16,000 British and Indian soldiers was wiped out. This was a terrible blow to the prestige of the British, and morale in the Bengal army sank lower.

In 1843 a new campaign was mounted for the conquest of Sind, but several sepoy regiments refused to march. This was because the foreign service allowances had been withdrawn. The Company was making new frontiers by its advances so that all service on the Indian subcontinent became 'home service'. The sepoys reasoned that service beyond the Indus River, a thousand miles from home, was sufficiently far away to justify the customary *batta* (allowance) which made so much difference to their pay. Mutinies

13

British soldiers crossing the River Sutlej during the first war against the Sikhs. A copy of a watercolour picture painted by a British officer, Lieutenant Henry Yule, in February 1846.

were often punished with great severity, but on this occasion British troops refused to act against the sepoys because it was clear that their grievance was a real one. Many English newspapers in India also supported the sepoys. The *Naval and Military Gazette* wrote, 'Whenever a mutiny occurs among the Bengal troops there has been some mismanagement either in the officers or in the Government.'

In 1845 the Sikhs from the Punjab invaded the Company's dominions. The fighting lasted less than two months but was the fiercest the Company's army had known. After another equally fierce war in 1849 the Punjab was finally annexed by the Company. Once again allowances for foreign service were withdrawn from the sepoys who had fought so bravely, and this resulted in further mutinies.

In 1852, again, troops ordered to go across the sea to Burma refused, though this time there was no severe punishment for the disobedience.

By the 1850s, when Britain was celebrating her industrial progress with the Great Exhibition of 1851 and involving herself in the heroic futilities of the Crimean War of 1854–6, the sepoys had become mistrustful and unhappy.

4 British 'improvements' and Indian traditions

In 1848 Lord Dalhousie had become Governor-General, and the annexation of the Punjab was part of his policy of governing forcefully. It was not only the sepoys, however, who were becoming exasperated. The British were trying to 'modernize' India, and all sections of Indian society, from the greatest to the humblest, were being affected by the high-handed and ruthless manner in which the 'improvements' were being enforced. In trying to create an efficient administration the British rode roughshod over the traditional customs of the people.

Princes and landowners were no longer secure in their territories. Dalhousie wished to 'tidy up' India by removing all the small states and permitting only the large ones to remain. Even the large ones, though nominally independent, would in fact be subject to British control. Much of this was done with good intentions, because some of the states were badly governed by their rulers and the peasant farmers were reduced to misery by harsh taxation demands on their crops. However, misrule by the princes was sometimes exaggerated by the British, merely to provide an

left: *1st Marquess of Dalhousie, 1812–60, painted by J. Watson-Gordon in 1847.*

right: *An Indian ruler in procession, dating from about 1770. The Mahratta chief Tuljaji is shown surrounded by his retainers.*

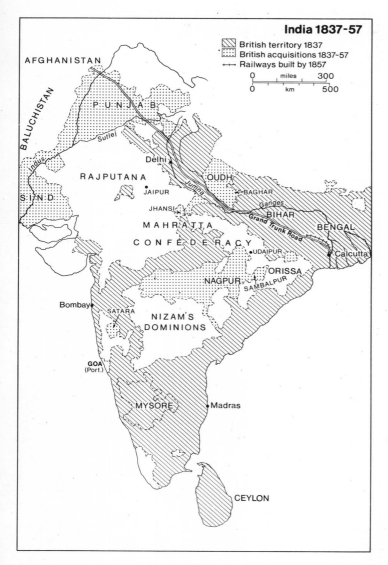

India 1837-57

British territory 1837
British acquisitions 1837-57
Railways built by 1857

miles 0 — 300
km 0 — 500

AFGHANISTAN

BALUCHISTAN

PUNJAB

Sutlej

Indus

SIND

RAJPUTANA

JAIPUR

Delhi

OUDH

Jumna

BAGHAR

JHANSI

Ganges

BIHAR

MAHRATTA

Grand Trunk Road

BENGAL

CONFEDERACY

Calcutta

UDAIPUR

ORISSA

NAGPUR

SAMBALPUR

Bombay

SATARA

NIZAM'S
DOMINIONS

GOA
(Port.)

MYSORE

Madras

CEYLON

overlord. This policy, known as 'the doctrine of lapse', brought in a rich crop of Hindu states: 1848 Satara, 1849 Jaipur and Sambalpur, 1850 Baghar, 1852 Udaipur, 1853 Jhansi, 1854 Nagpur.

The Muslim kingdom of Oudh had over the past ninety years become more and more enmeshed in British expansion. The kings of that important state had always kept their side of the many unequal treaties the Company imposed upon them and had permitted hundreds of thousands of their subjects over the years to enlist in the Bengal army. In 1856 Oudh was finally annexed on the grounds of misrule by the king. The charge was almost certainly true, but Dalhousie was breaking the treaties between Oudh and the British. The king's personal army of 60,000 troops was disbanded and they drifted back to their villages to spread disaffection against the Company. The great landowners of Oudh, who had always been semi-independent chieftains, were forbidden to fortify their castles or to arm their followers. Many landholders had their lands confiscated because they could not produce documents establishing their titles, though their families had held the land for many generations. The nobles and courtiers who had depended upon the King lost their livelihood. New taxes were imposed upon everyone.

Even kings who had lost their power and retained only a title and an income were not safe. Why, thought Dalhousie, should useless and expensive relics of the past be preserved? So the heir of the Mogul Emperor had to promise not to claim title or palace, and when the Mahratta Peishwa died his adopted heir, the Nana Sahib, was refused both the title and the pension which he had expected.

It may seem that Dalhousie was only curbing the rich and powerful, and this was not harming the ordinary poor Indians. Indeed, he was curbing the very people who had oppressed the poor – or so the British would have argued. But did the ordinary Indians see it that way? Where the British ruled, the land was divided into districts, and each district had officials appointed to rule it – which, in practice, meant collecting the taxes, keeping order and administering justice. When these officials were honest, intelligent and hard-working the people of the district probably found that their lives were a little less hard and that they could be sure of getting a fair hearing if they fell into trouble. But, as we

excuse for annexing territories. (As it turned out, British land taxation in some areas was high and so harshly enforced that despairing peasants abandoned their fields.)

If the ruler of any state had no heir, Dalhousie did not permit him to adopt one, although this was a time-honoured practice, recognized in Hindu law. When the ruler died, the Company seized his territory, on the pretext that it was the saw on page 16, there were times when the opposite happened. The most notorious example of British rule working to the disadvantage of the poorer people was the *zemindar* system. *Zemindars* were tax-collectors, or rather tax-farmers. They took the land tax and paid the government a fixed sum every year, each for his stretch of countryside. Tax-farming was understood in Europe, but there was one thing about this Indian system that the British found hard to grasp. The *zemindars* had a hereditary right to collect the taxes in their areas. So the British simplified the system to something they did understand. They recognized the *zemindars* as owners of the land for which they paid taxes, and the peasants as being no more than tenants. The *zemindars* now had the chance to squeeze their peasants as hard as they pleased, and many took the opportunity. At the same time, because the peasants had to find money even in years when the harvest was bad, many of them had to borrow, and fell into the clutches of village money-lenders. This system originated in Bengal, but spread to other parts of India.

To the peasants, who made up about two-thirds of the population of India, it does not seem likely that British 'improvements' meant much. What use had they for the first railways and the telegraph that were beginning to link the parts of India? Perhaps they would be grateful if they were protected from tax-collectors, landlords and money-lenders, but the British officials often failed to give this protection, which was the main thing the peasants needed.

Did the fate of their kings mean anything to these millions of poor people whose lives were filled by a never-ending struggle to grow enough food for themselves and their masters, with the threat of starvation constantly in the background? We cannot tell much of what they thought in the villages then, but there is no doubt that very many Indians were devoted to their traditional beliefs, their customs and leaders, and that they felt insulted when they saw or heard how the brash British were sweeping aside the old order.

Little attempt was made by the British, many of whom could not speak the local languages, to understand the customs and feelings of the people. Lord Macaulay recognized that 'respect must be paid to feelings generated by differences of religions, of nation and of caste', but the

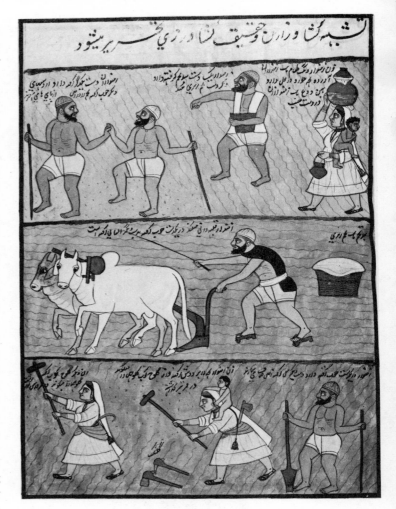

This Kashmiri painting of the 1850s gives a good impression of the agricultural tasks which occupied most Indians for all their lives.

attitude of William Wilberforce (the great leader of the anti-slavery movement) seems to have been more typical, when he talked of 'the vast superiority even of European laws and institutions, and far more of British institutions, over those of Asia'. Many Indians believed that their religion was being threatened and that the British intended to force Christianity upon them. There were reasons for them

This lively painting, made in 1800, illustrates the Indian custom of suttee (the word sati means 'a true lady'). Some of the higher castes among the Hindus permitted or persuaded widows to burn themselves on the funeral pyres of their dead husbands.

The thuggees (deceivers) joined parties of travellers on the roads. They strangled their victims with silk scarves and buried them in shallow graves in woods or groves near the camps. This drawing was said to be accurate by thuggees who had been arrested.

to think this; some military and civilian officials openly encouraged the Bible and disparaged the holy books of India. Some Indian customs had been suppressed. One of these was *thuggee*, a cult of ritual murderers who for centuries had killed harmless travellers in the name of Kali, the goddess of destruction. Another was *suttee*, the custom of burning Hindu widows on the funeral pyres of their husbands. Another was the killing of female babies to avoid the expense of marriage dowries. These were regarded by the British as crimes. They were all corruptions of the Hindu religion, which many Hindu reformers were preaching against as evils which ought to be suppressed. However, the British began to form the impression that all the Indian people were savages, and that the whole of Hindu religion was false and evil.

In the British Parliament, also, many evangelical members spoke of the necessity of establishing Christianity in India. Indians who had become suspicious saw a sinister meaning in things which, to the British, were quite unconnected with religion. Railways and telegraph seemed to orthodox Hindus part of the westernizing process which

Travel by steamship: sepoys being carried up the Indus in a covered 'flat'. Watercolour by J. B. Bellasis, 1856.

would eventually level all society and destroy the differences of caste. Equality before the law appeared obviously fair and just to the British; but it meant that the highest Brahmin and lowest Untouchable were placed on the same level, and this was a threat to the traditional ordering of Hindu society.

In the Bengal army there had long been suspicion among the sepoys that the British were not impartial about religion. This was not only caused by the frequent disputes about overseas service, but also by the failure of the officers to understand the ritual importance of food and cooking and of certain habits of hygiene. Innovations in uniform, like the forbidding of caste marks, the cutting of hair, the wearing of leather (forbidden to Hindus) and so on, all produced uneasiness and sometimes mutiny. The sepoys were mistaken in suspecting that there was any positive policy to change their religion, but equally the British were wrong in failing to appreciate the importance of caste to their men. In Hinduism if a man's caste is broken he is removed utterly from all contact with his family and people, and will suffer in the next life horrors which are infinitely worse than any Hell.

Many of the sepoys were Brahmins, that is of the highest caste, and any apparent attack on their religion affected them most seriously.

Muslim sepoys too were worried and annoyed. Though they were not affected by the complications of caste, they could not help wondering if their own religion was being threatened. They were proud of their religion, and proud that the last great rulers of India, the Moguls, had been Muslims. Above all, many of them came from the Muslim kingdom of Oudh. Not only were they offended at the way their king had been treated, but they lost special privileges that they had enjoyed as long as they had been subjects of an independent state.

Looking back, it is easy for the historian to see the dangers in the situation. The self-confident British, convinced of their own rightness, failed to sense the mood they were creating among the people they depended on.

5 The greased cartridge

It was the introduction into the army of the new Enfield rifle, a longer-range and more accurate weapon, and with it a new cartridge, which in 1857 provided the spark which set the dry tinder of discontent on fire. For the new rifle both powder and bullet were enclosed in a paper cartridge which was greased to keep its contents dry. In order to load the weapon, the cartridge was pulled open in the soldiers' teeth and its contents rammed into the rifle. The sepoys believed that the grease was made of a mixture of cow and pig fat, and so some of it probably was. The cow is sacred to the Hindus and the pig abominable to Muslims, so a more offensive mixture could hardly have been invented for an army consisting almost entirely of Hindus and Muslims. The authorities intended no offence: other kinds of grease were used as well, beeswax and mutton fat for instance, and the new cartridge was still 'experimental' and had not been made available everywhere. But it was yet another example of the failure of the British to take the religious beliefs of the sepoys seriously.

The British, full of confidence in their own racial and cultural superiority, did not appreciate that their drinking of alcohol, their eating of pork and beef and many of their other habits and customs filled both Hindus and Muslims with revulsion and horror. A century before, many British officials and officers had respected the Indians with whom they had dealings. Now they thought of themselves as masters, and few of them made any effort to understand how the natives thought about life.

Strange signs and omens began to appear. It was said that calves were born with two heads or six legs and huge flocks of ravens circulated in the skies, signalling doom and death. Religious teachers foretold that the downfall of the British would happen exactly one hundred years after the battle of Plassey. Small, flat wheat cakes called *chapattis* were circu-lated from village to village and into the sepoys' barracks. No one knew what message they brought but all believed it was a sign of war. Agents of the king of Oudh and of the old and powerless Emperor in Delhi spread rumours that cows' bones and pigs' bones had been ground up and put into the sepoys' flour ration. Others whispered that the Persians and Russians had combined with the Afghans and that together they would drive the British out of India. So rumour, terror, anger and superstition blew like a devil's wind across the sun-struck plains of northern India.

In February 1857 a sepoy regiment refused to accept the new cartridges and they were disarmed and disbanded at Barrackpore, near Calcutta. In the same place, in March, a Brahmin sepoy named Mangal Pandy, calling upon his com-rades to rise in defence of their religion, ran amok and shot the British adjutant; he was arrested, court-martialled and hanged. In spite of these signs, neither the civil nor military authorities believed in the possibility of a general revolt. The commander-in-chief moved off to Simla with his staff to pass the 'hot weather' period in the cool hill-station there.

At this time other commitments elsewhere in Asia had reduced the numbers of British soldiers in India to about 40,000, whereas there were 300,000 sepoys. Between Cal-cutta and Peshawar there were only four British infantry regiments, one cavalry regiment and a few companies of artillery, ready for immediate action. Most of the senior officers, after many years' service in India, were old and unfit for command. The only region where there were strong British units was the recently annexed Punjab, whose war-like inhabitants had nearly beaten the British only a few years before.

As the weather became hotter and men's tempers shorter all the resentments caused by their real and imagined griev-ances brought the anger of the sepoys to an uncontrollable

The Enfield rifle

This percussion-lock rifle was produced in the British Ordnance Factory at Enfield near London. It came into use in the British army in 1853. Shortly afterwards it was sent out for trials for the Company army in India. The 'rifling' on the inside of the barrel made the shot more accurate and gave the weapon a greater range. It was an enormous improvement on the Brown Bess smooth-bore flintlock musket which had been the standard weapon of all British forces since the early eighteenth century.

A greased cartridge

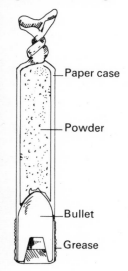

- Paper case
- Powder
- Bullet
- Grease

How it was loaded

1.
The soldier tears open the end of the cartridge with his teeth.

2.
He pours the powder down the muzzle of his rifle. Then he thrusts the bullet, still wrapped in the cartridge paper which makes it a tight fit, into the muzzle.

3.
He takes his ramrod from its slot beneath the rifle barrel, and rams paper, bullet and powder to the bottom of the barrel.

pitch. The Emperor Bahadur Shah in Delhi, who was almost a prisoner of the British, was also a poet. Among his many verses on themes of courtly love and warlike deeds he wrote this little comment on the passing scene:

'Na Iran ne Kiya na Shah Russ ne
  Angrej Ko tabah Kiya Kartosh ne.'
'Nor Persian war nor even Russian Tsar e'er did
  As much to break the English as the cartridge did.'

6 The outbreak of mutiny and the struggle for Delhi

The outbreak

Meerut was an important garrison town some 50 miles (80 km) north-east of Delhi. It was unique in India in that here the British troops, a regiment of infantry and one of cavalry, were almost equal in numbers to the sepoys and were considerably strengthened by at least twelve guns. This suggests that, even though the sepoys all over northern India were ripe for mutiny, the outbreak cannot have been fully planned or organized.

On 23 April 1857, eighty-five members of a sepoy cavalry regiment refused to accept the cartridges. A court-martial composed of Indian officers sentenced them to long terms of imprisonment. On 9 May the British commander ordered them to be paraded in their chains in front of the whole garrison. The next day, a Sunday, while most of the British were at church parade, the sepoys broke out into open revolt. They had heard rumours that the British were coming to kill them. They broke open the jail, released the prisoners, burned houses and killed some British officers and their families. While they ran about in disorder, cries of 'Remember Mangal Pandy' could be heard in the smoke and fire.

The British commanders were so surprised by what had happened that they took no action at all and the mutineers left Meerut and moved off towards Delhi. In spite of the fact that there was a British cavalry regiment at Meerut, the mutineers were not pursued. When they reached Delhi they crossed the Jumna River on a bridge of boats tied together and appeared under the window of the Mogul Emperor in the palace of the Red Fort. They shouted for him to show himself and to accept their salutes as the Emperor of all Hindustan. In Delhi there was a garrison of three regiments of sepoys and some artillery, and these now joined the mutiny, proclaiming the Emperor. Bahadur Shah's own retainers, of course, also proclaimed him Emperor.

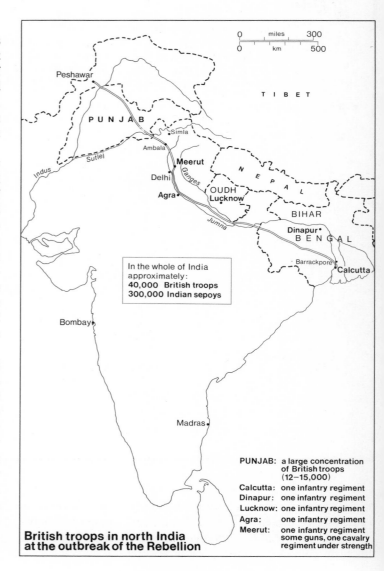

In the whole of India approximately:
40,000 British troops
300,000 Indian sepoys

PUNJAB: a large concentration of British troops (12–15,000)
Calcutta: one infantry regiment
Dinapur: one infantry regiment
Lucknow: one infantry regiment
Agra: one infantry regiment
Meerut: one infantry regiment some guns, one cavalry regiment under strength

British troops in north India at the outbreak of the Rebellion

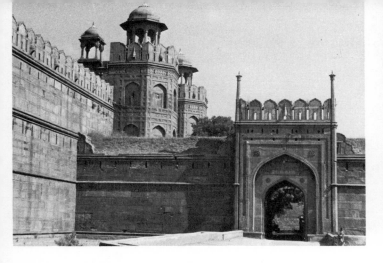

There was nothing that the few British officers could do. Some of them blew up the gunpowder in the magazine to prevent it falling into the hands of the sepoys and lost their lives in doing so. There were still, however, large quantities of powder and ammunition in Delhi and in the main magazine outside the city. The remaining Europeans were hunted down and either killed or imprisoned in the palace. Only a few escaped. There was no telegraph to Simla, where the British commander-in-chief was, but a message telling of the mutiny was sent on 11 May to Ambala by the courageous operator, before he and the telegraph office fell into the hands of the mutineers.

The people of Delhi looked upon the sepoys as liberators, and old Bahadur Shah, too, was pleased. He knew, as we saw on page 16, that the British intended him to be the last of the Moguls. Sitting on his polished marble throne, now perhaps he hoped and dreamed a poet's dream that his noble line might be great once more. The sepoys, though, showed more inclination to live at the expense of the citizens and to quarrel among themselves than to venture out very often to attack the British.

As the summer went on and food and money became short and the sepoys more unruly, the old Emperor, now virtually their prisoner without honour even in his own palace, retired to his private rooms and threatened to leave the city to become a hermit. In the Great Mosque, the Jama Masjid, the Muslims raised the green flag of Holy War against all infidels, and tensions developed between Mus-

above: *Part of the palace of the Red Fort at Delhi, built by the Mogul Emperor Shah Jahan between 1640 and 1648. The marble throne is in the special royal apartments. It replaced the peacock throne which the Emperor Shah Jahan had made and which was seized by the King of Persia in 1739. On this throne sat the last Mogul, Bahadur Shah.*

below: *The gateway of the old magazine at Delhi. Above the centre can be seen the memorial tablet to Lieutenant Willoughby and the eight soldiers who defended it and finally blew it up.*

lims and Hindus. The sepoys could not agree upon their strategy and they had a succession of inexperienced leaders. The British prisoners in the palace were murdered, against the orders of the Emperor, and the liberation of Delhi was beginning to go sour.

The recapture of Delhi

On 12 May, when the commander-in-chief heard of the situation in Delhi, he ordered what British forces were available to assemble at Ambala and move to the recapture of the city. There were some horse artillery, a cavalry and an infantry regiment of the Royal Army and two British regiments of the Company's Bengal army. There were also some cavalry and infantry regiments of sepoys, one of which mutinied and fled to join the rebels at Delhi while the others were disarmed and disbanded. Then there was a delay. Government economies had reduced supplies and transport. There was not enough ammunition for the infantry, none for the guns and no bullocks to pull them. But the position was critical and delay might be fatal. Already news was coming in that mutinies were erupting all across northern India, and at all costs the British must hit back and regain the ancient capital. A small British force with some loyal Indian cavalry had already begun to march on Delhi from Meerut, and the Ambala troops joined them late in May.

A few miles outside, at a place called Badli-ki-Serai, was an army of 30,000 mutineers and other rebels, strongly entrenched and supported by thirty guns. On 8 June, though heavily outnumbered, the British attacked them and drove them from their positions and chased them into the city.

Just to the north-west of Delhi there lies a stretch of high ground known as the Ridge, and here the British established their camp. The city was an awe-inspiring objective for so small an army. Its heavily fortified walls extended for more than 6 miles (10 km) and on the east it was moated by the Jumna River. There were ten strongly defended gates and many bastions with at least ten guns mounted in each. Inside was a big force – nobody could be sure how big – of well-armed sepoys and others who had joined them. The British outside had under 3,000 men and twenty-four light field-guns.

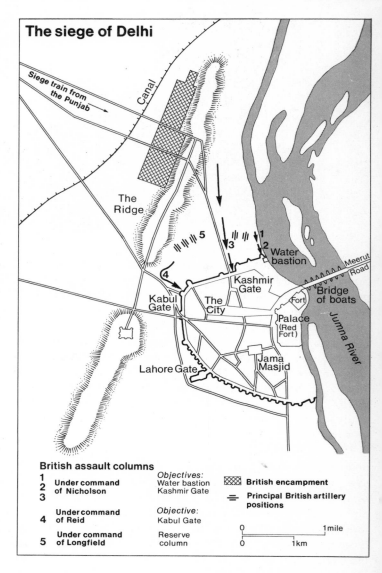

The siege of Delhi

British assault columns
1 2 3	Under command of Nicholson	*Objectives:* Water bastion Kashmir Gate
4	Under command of Reid	*Objective:* Kabul Gate
5	Under command of Longfield	Reserve column

▨ British encampment
═ Principal British artillery positions

Lord Canning, the Governor-General who had succeeded Dalhousie in 1856, urged the speedy recapture of Delhi. But the attack was delayed long enough to permit large numbers of mutineers from other places to enter the city, so that a British assault would be suicidal until reinforcements reached them too. On 23 June, the hundredth anniversary of Plassey, the rebels made an attack on the British positions

John Nicholson, 1822–57. Painting by C. Vivian.

The siege train on its way from the Punjab to Delhi, painted by Captain G. F. Atkinson of the Bengal Engineers, who was an eyewitness.

but were thrown back in confusion. The British were losing many men, mainly through cholera (up to 450 in one week), but they were also getting reinforcements which had raised their number to 7,000 by now.

Everything depended on what happened in the Punjab. If the sepoys there mutinied, and if the warlike Sikhs joined them and rose against the British who had so recently begun to rule their land, not only Delhi but the whole of north-west India would surely be lost to the British. The sepoys in the Punjab mutinied, or tried to. The Sikhs stood by the British. The British officers and officials who had been sent to the Punjab and the North-West Frontier during the past few years had been men of outstanding character. Some, like John Nicholson for example, had become almost legendary heroes to the people among whom they worked and fought. It has been argued that it was the strength and fairness of those men in the years before 1857 that saved the British in India.

Now Nicholson was on his way to help, with 4,000 men. A rather larger force of rebels left Delhi to intercept him, but Nicholson routed them, took all their guns and killed

800. (There was no question of taking prisoners – death was the only answer to sepoys who broke their oaths of loyalty and murdered those who had trusted them. So the British thought, and it seems that there were many Indians who agreed.)

Though the British on the Ridge were growing stronger, Delhi's defences were as formidable as ever. They could not be broken without heavy guns. So the men on the Ridge had to wait, suffering many more casualties from cholera, until early September when the siege train from the Punjab arrived, consisting of heavy guns drawn by elephants and hundreds of bullock carts loaded with powder and shot, 'enough to grind Delhi to powder'. As the guns were placed in position to batter the walls and gates, five assault columns were organized, each of about 1,000 men. About half of these men were Indian soldiers.

The assault commenced on the morning of 14 September, and by evening some of the British forces were inside the city. It had cost them 1,200 dead and wounded. Nicholson was mortally wounded leading an attack on the Lahore Gate. Another important objective, the Kashmir Gate, was

above: *The British gun positions on the Ridge, north-west of Delhi, painted by Captain Atkinson. Several of the gunners are resting, exhausted by their hard labour in the heat.*

The Kashmir gate. The engraving above is a contemporary artist's impression of the British attack. The photograph on the right shows the remains in 1974, still standing despite the siege.

carried by the 60th Rifles and the Sirmur Company of Gurkhas, but with great loss to themselves.

That night the British troops inside the city began looting and killing indiscriminately. The soldiers had found a large quantity of liquor and they drank it like water. It was said that the mutineers, knowing the weakness of British soldiers in these circumstances, left the drink deliberately. But they did not take the opportunity to counterattack. There was a lull in the fighting for more than a day, and some of the mutineers and many of the civilian population fled from the city.

When the attack was resumed the British had to fight hard from house to house. Delhi was a network of little alleyways and streets with high-walled houses and courtyards. It was like a heavily defended maze, but the attackers knew that they were winning and drove savagely forward. On 18 September the Emperor fled, and three days later the British fired a salute of guns to signal the complete recapture of Delhi. It was of the greatest importance, for many people would think that if the British could regain Delhi it was only a matter of time before they crushed the rebels everywhere.

Meanwhile, the victors had some accounts to settle. The Emperor was pursued by cavalry, surrendered on the promise that his life would be spared, and was brought back to Delhi a prisoner; but his three sons were killed in cold blood. From the city thousands of civilians had to leave everything and flee for their lives, but thousands of others were not so lucky. Innocent though most of them were, they paid a hundred times over for the murder of the British prisoners. This was not British justice, it was bloody vengeance.

The last Mogul Emperor, Bahadur Shah, surrenders to Hodson, a famous British leader of Indian cavalry, after the British recapture Delhi. A print from a British history of the Rebellion by C. Ball, published in 1859.

7 The spread of the Rebellion and the struggle for Oudh

While the fighting at Delhi had been going on, sepoys had mutinied in most of the garrisons that spread across northern India, dotted about the Ganges valley and near the Grand Trunk Road that crossed the plains all the way from Bengal to the frontier of Afghanistan. In some places the mutinies were nipped in the bud, the sepoys disarmed before they made up their minds to revolt. In other places, though, not only the sepoys rose but also great numbers of the local people who wanted to get rid of the British. The British were taken by surprise and their forces were stretched to the limit. But they were not destroyed, they got over the first shock, they struck back and in the end they won. What made this possible, in the face of what at first sight seems an impossible situation for the British?

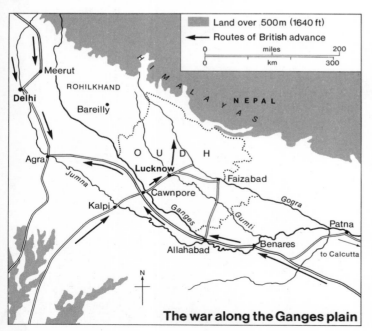

The war along the Ganges plain

We have already seen part of the explanation at Delhi. The mutineers had no real plans and no leader, while the British had a clear objective and regular commanders. The rebels argued and quarrelled while the British were under a united command. Besides, many Indians were fighting at the side of the British.

Most of the population of India, in fact, did not revolt. In the Bombay and Madras armies there were practically no mutinies. This may have been because there were fewer high-caste Hindus in their ranks, and they were less sensitive about possible threats to their religious purity. Besides, there had been considerably less political upset of the Oudh type in southern and central India, so these sepoys were not so torn by conflicts of loyalties.

Though, as we shall see, some Indian rulers – or, more usually, ex-rulers – took this opportunity to revolt, most of them preferred to support the British, sometimes even sending their own troops against the rebels. The British were also fortunate that neighbouring rulers did not try to take advantage of their difficulties. Persia and Afghanistan, though both had recently been at war with the British, remained aloof, and the king of Nepal sent 10,000 Gurkhas to help the British.

Not only rulers and their men supported the British. In the towns most merchants and money-lenders thought that the Company's rule gave them peace and helped them to prosper; many, indeed, had made good profits in land as a result of the Company's policies. There were also some lawyers and minor officials who had learnt British ways and who made a good living by serving the Company's administration. People like this could see little good in the revolts, and continued to work as usual.

It is possible that most of the people were surprised and confused when the mutinies broke out. Where British officials were killed or fled to save themselves, much of the countryside was left in turmoil. Small bands of sepoys roamed the districts robbing the peasant farmers. Tribal and religious disputes broke out among different groups of Indians and old rivalries were renewed. In some places it was every man for himself, and everyone's hand was turned against his neighbour.

The Rebellion of 1857 was the reaction of many people who felt that their ways of life were threatened by change. Because it was not planned and organized, outbursts in different places did not join together effectively. It is clear that various groups and individuals were acting for their own interests or for what they themselves held sacred. They joined forces when it suited them, but not because they were devoted to one great common cause. Least of all did they conceive of India as a whole, as a motherland waiting to be made free and united. Therefore it is not correct to consider the Rebellion as a national movement for independence. The idea of Indian nationhood was to come much later.

Against the numerous but ill-coordinated risings, then, the Company authorities had many advantages. Their great disadvantage was the small number of British troops, either Company or Royal, that they could use when the trouble began. This weakness, however, was only temporary. A war in Persia had just ended, and troops were on their way back to their normal stations in India. A war in China had just begun, and troops from Britain were sailing there; they could easily be, and were, ordered to pause in India. Unless the rebels could win quickly, the balance would swing ever more heavily against them.

Apart from Delhi, the fiercest fighting in the summer of 1857 centred in a part of the Ganges valley where the Company's policies had been especially resented: Oudh. As if the situation were not sufficiently dangerous already, a British commander aroused even more hostility in that area by his blundering harshness. When the mutinies broke out Colonel Neill had just taken command of a Company British regiment back from Persia. He was sent from Calcutta with orders to secure the strategic river city of Allahabad with its huge fortress. In spite of its importance, there were no British troops in the garrison there. By 3 June Neill reached Benares, and hot-headedly insisted on disarming the sepoy regiments there, for fear they might joint the mutinies. The

business was mismanaged and finally artillery opened fire on the sepoys. On 9 June Neill moved on.

Allahabad had been quiet, and a sepoy regiment stationed there had volunteered to march against the rebels at Delhi. Then news came of the slaughter of the Benares sepoys, and the Allahabad sepoys were thrown into alarm and confusion. There was a parade on the evening of 6 June, called so that the sepoys could receive the thanks of the commander-in-chief for volunteering to help at Delhi. After this parade the sepoys mutinied and killed their officers. Soon mobs were running wild in the city, murdering British people, looting and burning. Neill arrived on 11 June, in time to prevent the fortress from being occupied by rebels. On his march from Benares he had burned villages indiscriminately, and the countryside around was in revolt. So it became impossible to send reinforcements in time to save the British in Cawnpore and Lucknow from being cut off by rebels. Neill meanwhile carried on with his policy of terror. He could not see that if anything were needed to drive into revolt those sepoys who had been wavering between loyalty and mutiny, it was brutality of this sort.

The Cawnpore massacre

Cawnpore, sometimes now spelt Kanpur, was the headquarters of the military command of the recently annexed province of Oudh. It was an important port on the Ganges which, until the railways were to be developed, was the chief trade route to Calcutta. General Sir Hugh Wheeler, who had already spent fifty years in India, was the commander of the garrison, which consisted of only a few British artillerymen and an overwhelming number of sepoys. There were also many British civilians in the town: merchants and their families and railway engineers working on the new line from Calcutta. Wheeler suspected the possibility of mutiny and knew that his main problem would be to protect the civilians. He busied himself preparing a fortified place to shelter these civilians near the river. Then, if necessary, they could escape by boat to Allahabad or Calcutta.

Living near Cawnpore was an Indian prince who had no reason to love the British. He was the Nana Sahib (page 16). He managed to conceal his hostility though, and in the early days of the Rebellion agreed to a British request to supply troops to guard the treasury. When the sepoys in Cawnpore mutinied on 4 June the Nana Sahib threw in his lot with them and managed, through his agents, to persuade the mutineers to attack the British in Cawnpore instead of marching off to Delhi. Most of the population in the district around Cawnpore also rose against the British, because of the severity of the land taxes. Even Indian officials of the Company joined in the revolt. The Nana Sahib set up his own government and on 20 June had himself proclaimed Peishwa.

The British held their entrenchments for three weeks without much difficulty. It was the heat and the shortage of water and food which forced them to surrender in the end. Terms were agreed on 26 June that they should leave their entrenchments and go to the Sati Chaura Ghat, a landing-place on the river, where boats would be provided to take them without harm to Allahabad. Some hundreds of British men, women and children left for the Ghat in carts supplied by the Nana Sahib on the morning of 27 June. A large crowd of jeering sepoys and townspeople came to see them off. They got safely into the boats. Then a signal was given and they were shot down from all sides. About 200 women and children were saved from the massacre, and the Nana Sahib ordered them to be imprisoned in a house in the town, where they suffered great hardship.

Help was on its way. A small British force under General Havelock marched from Allahabad, defeated the Nana Sahib's troops and entered Cawnpore on 17 July. But they rescued no one. On the previous day orders had been given to the mutineers in Cawnpore that the British women and children should be killed. The sepoys refused to do it, so

below: Down the steps of the Sati Chaura Ghat the exhausted British made their way into their boats, while the crowd jeered. A few minutes later the sepoys opened fire, killing most of them.

right: The house at Cawnpore where the British women and children were massacred. In this contemporary painting by R. H. Sankey the mess has been cleared away and the soldiers are talking quietly about the terrible event.

butchers were sent in with knives. All the women and children were hacked to death and their remains thrown down a well.

It was this horrible deed, more than anything else, that ensured that there could be no reconciliation between the British and the rebels.

The anger of the British at the Cawnpore massacre produced an orgy of hatred and revenge. Justice and reason were forgotten. The innocent as well as the guilty were pursued and punished. The British in India felt themselves surrounded by countless diabolical enemies and threatened with extinction, and they struck back with cruelty born of terror. One reason why the rebels often went on fighting when they knew they had lost was because they knew that they would not receive mercy or even a fair trial. It was better to die fighting than to be hanged in a pigskin or to be blown to pieces from the mouth of a gun. The madness which affected everyone that summer produced in the British and the mutineers equal anger and fear. Men of both nations who were usually respectful of women, loving to children and careful of the weak, became merciless killers.

left: *This engraving illustrates the way the British public imagined their heroic and virtuous womenfolk being attacked. It is supposed to represent Miss Wheeler shooting a mutineer, although there is no evidence that the incident ever happened.*

above: *'Justice'. The British attitude was probably best shown by a series of cartoons in* Punch, *the so-called 'Cawnpore' cartoons. The cartoonist carefully emphasizes that the British spare women and children.*

The Residency in Lucknow as sketched by Lieutenant C. H. Meecham in 1858, before and after the fierce bombardment. The ruins still stand today, a reminder of those who died on both sides.

The siege at Lucknow

Lucknow was the capital of the Muslim kingdom of Oudh, and was full of magnificent mosques and palaces, some of which still stand. The home of the senior British official, the Residency, became the fortified centre of resistance to the rebels. As Cawnpore became for the British the symbol of rebel treachery and cruelty, so Lucknow became the symbol of their own heroism.

The commander at Lucknow was Sir Henry Lawrence. A week before the mutiny at Meerut a regiment of his sepoys

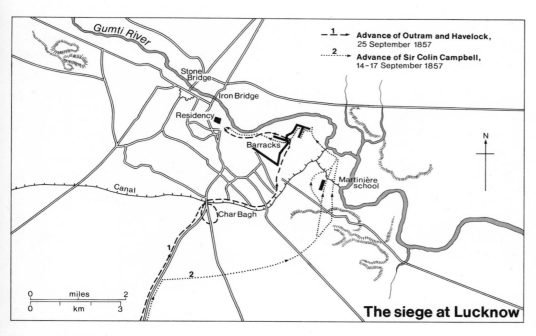

1 ⟶ **Advance of Outram and Havelock,**
25 September 1857

2 ⟶ **Advance of Sir Colin Campbell,**
14–17 September 1857

Gumti River

Stone Bridge

Iron Bridge

Residency

Barracks

Canal

Char Bagh

Martinière school

N

miles 2
km 3

The siege at Lucknow

below: *Lucknow was a very widespread city with buildings separated by large open areas and park lands. This picture, also by Meecham, shows some of the British gun positions.*

refused to accept the new cartridges and were disarmed. For some years Lawrence had warned his superiors of the inevitability of rebellion if they continued their policies, and after this incident he began to prepare the Residency to withstand an attack. On the evening of 30 May a disturbance started in Lucknow. A British regiment of the Royal Army, under Lawrence's strong leadership, put it down quickly and prevented a massacre. However, in the rest of Oudh most of the towns had fallen to the mutineers, which made it possible for thousands of rebels to flood into the area of Lucknow.

The queen, or Begum, of Oudh took control of the Rebellion in the name of her dispossessed husband, the Nawab, who was a prisoner of the British in Calcutta.

By the middle of June only the Residency area and part of the nearby Martinière school remained in British hands. Lawrence decided that attack was the best form of defence and sent his troops to try to disperse rebel forces outside Lucknow. He had underestimated the strength and determination of the rebels. The British were badly beaten, and the survivors fell back on the Residency. Lawrence's mistake had encouraged the enemy and weakened his own side,

almost undoing the effect of his earlier preparations. There were 3,000 British and Indians inside the Residency, of whom less than half were able to fight. Surrounding them were hundreds of thousands of hostile people and tens of

far left: *British soldiers and volunteers are shown in this Meecham picture digging a tunnel in the floor of a building in Lucknow, attempting to locate and destroy the besiegers' mines.*

left: *Sir Henry Havelock, 1795–1857.*

thousands of armed men. On 2 July Lawrence was mortally wounded by a shell and died two days later. Colonel Inglis now took command.

General Havelock, on reaching Cawnpore (page 30), heard of Lawrence's death and decided to move quickly to relieve Lucknow. Leaving a small force in Cawnpore, he advanced across the Ganges, and by 25 July was in a position to fight his way to Lucknow. This effort was wasted, however, because he had to fall back again and recross the river; he had heard of strong rebel activity near his base at Cawnpore, his men were ill and he was running short of munitions. Though Havelock had no choice, his retreat made the British seem weak. Some of the land-owners of Oudh who had been hesitating now joined the Rebellion. In this kingdom, at least, the military mutiny began to look like a national uprising, with the whole people at war against the British.

In the Residency about 700 British and Indians now had to withstand furious assaults of ten times that number of sepoys and townspeople. Muslim and Hindu religious leaders were working up their followers into a state of frenzy. Night and day the drums were beating and the war hymns sounding. The noise of shot and shell was deafening and the Residency buildings were riddled with holes. A pall of

smoke hung over the city and the cries and shouts of the opposing armies filled the air. The boys of the Martinière school, in their own post, stood side by side with the British, Sikh and other Indian soldiers and defended the chief bastions with rifle and musket fire. Time and again the rebels, howling defiance, hurled themselves forward with reckless bravery, but were thrown back. The siege lasted nearly three months and during that time four all-out attacks and countless sudden rushes were repelled by the defenders. All the time the Union Jack fluttered over the shattered Residency.

In mid-September Sir James Outram, who had come from Persia to take command in India, reached Cawnpore with reinforcements. He and Havelock decided to push on for Lucknow at once with 3,000 men. In the Residency Colonel Inglis had supplies for only ten more days. On 25 September Outram and Havelock cut their way into the Residency with the loss of half their force, but they were too weakened to break out again. The siege continued.

Now all hopes were placed on Sir Colin Campbell, who was advancing from Cawnpore with a new relieving force of 4,000. On 14 November he arrived at the outskirts of Lucknow. In the Residency a civilian clerk called Kavanagh, who was of mixed British and Indian descent,

right: *Sir Colin Campbell, 1792–1863, Commander-in-Chief of the British forces in India.*

far right: *This photograph, taken after the British recaptured Lucknow, shows T. H. Kavanagh (in a white hat) sitting among his comrades.*

volunteered to take messages to Campbell informing him of the situation and supplying the code to be used for semaphore signals. He disguised himself as an Indian and made his way through the rebel lines. Campbell's army advanced and took the Martinière school, and from here rebel strongholds were attacked by Scottish Highlanders and Sikhs from the Punjab. On 17 November the relief succeeded and the defenders of the Residency were rescued, though it took months more of hard fighting before the rebel armies in the Lucknow–Cawnpore area were really beaten. It was not until March 1858 that Lucknow was finally captured.

Havelock died at the moment of victory. Kavanagh was awarded the Victoria Cross, the highest British award for bravery. He was the first of very few civilians ever to receive it. The boys of the Martinière school were awarded the Mutiny Medal, 'Defence of Lucknow', and the school itself was granted a Battle Honour. It is the only school in the world to have one.

Many personal accounts, letters and diaries, survive of the siege. This chapter ends with a page from *The Chronicle of Private Henry Metcalfe*, one example of an ordinary soldier's experience of the horrors in which he was involved.

This extraordinary house was built by a French soldier of fortune, Martin, who became a major-general in the service of the East India Company. It was completed in 1795. Martin left it in his will to be a school for Anglo-Indian boys. It still flourishes as the Martinière school.

There was one young lad in the Band named Symes. His mother, step-father, sister and brother were butchered at Cawnpore. I was by when he heard the news. I thought the poor young fellow's heart broke on the spot. However, he made a sort of vow that when he had a chance he would neither spare man, woman or child on account of his family being slain. However, on the morning after Havelock's force came in there were volunteers asked for, to go and clear the position of any of the enemy who were thought to be still in position around us. Well this young lad happened to be of the party, as also myself. After we had been out some time I missed this young fellow. I asked if anyone knew what became of him. One man told me he had seen him rush into a house close by, pointing to the house. I thought, strange, that the young lad did not come out of the house again, so I made a rush towards the house and I heard a scuffle going on. I rushed in and saw the lad in a very awkward position. A huge Sepoy had a hold of the lad's musket and was in the act of cutting at him with his Tulwar, or native sword. I just arrived in time to save him. He said to me, "Oh, Harry, I am a brute." I said, "How is that Jack?" He said, "Oh, I said when I came out I would spare no one, and I fired at a young woman and I am afraid I killed her, and by so doing I have placed myself on a par with the rebels by me killing her. I will not get my own relatives restored to me and consequently I am not fit to be called a soldier or a Christian." I rallied him on it and said perhaps he had not killed her, but it was no use. I asked him to point out the spot where this took place. He did so, and on going towards the spot we saw some of our men stooping over someone who was laying down. When we got to the spot we found it to be the young woman who the young lad had fired at. She was slightly wounded and had fainted, and in this position our men had found her, and seeing her seemingly all right this young lad almost jumped for joy at the thought of him not killing her. A few men brought this poor young native woman into the Garrison and had her wound dressed, and she was then sent about her business, a striking contrast to the way our poor women and children were treated, but then we were soldiers – they were fiends.

8 The later stages of the Rebellion

By the spring of 1858 the British had Delhi firmly in their grasp and had broken up the main rebel armies in Oudh. There was still a great deal of hard fighting to be done but, as reinforcements came in, they could concentrate on the two other areas where rebellion seemed to have taken a firm hold. One of these was to the north in Rohilkhand, a hilly land with a warlike Muslim population. These people were inspired by a religious leader, the Maulvi of Faizabad, who had escaped from Lucknow with many of his followers. Sir Colin Campbell sent a strong force in pursuit, and it smashed the rebel army of Rohilkhand at Bareilly on 5 May 1858. But the Maulvi remained at large, and proved to be a leader of unusual ability. He was a great trouble to the British until he made the mistake of trying to enter a stronghold where the Raja preferred the British. As the Maulvi came forward, mounted on an elephant, he was shot dead. After this the Rebellion in that part of India soon died away.

The Rani of Jhansi

The other area of rebellion lay to the south of the Ganges plain, in the northern part of central India.

It was a wild, mountainous and forested area dotted with the rock fortresses of warring chieftains. The British controlled the region by alliances with the chief princes. One of these, the Maharaja of Gwalior, remained on the side of the British throughout the Rebellion. The great fort at Gwalior

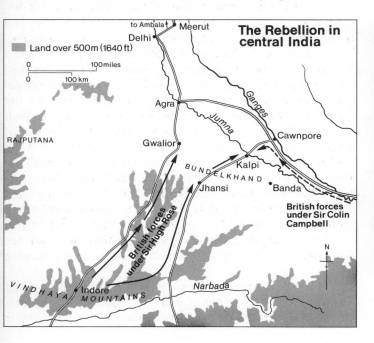

This portrait of the Rani of Jhansi was painted in watercolour on ivory, soon after her death. No true portrait from life is known to exist.

left: *Horse artillery,
depicted by Atkinson.
This picture gives a sense
of the urgency of much of
the campaigning.*

below left: *Tantia Topi,
sketched just before his
execution, by Captain
C. R. Baugh, 1859.*

is one of the most remarkable of all the strongholds in India.

Another of the royal persons with whom the British had an alliance was the queen of Jhansi, the Rani Laksmi Bai. On the death of the Raja in 1854 the British, by Dalhousie's 'doctrine of lapse' (see page 16), absorbed Jhansi because there was no heir to the state. The Rani appealed to Britain but in spite of this her kingdom was forfeited and the Company began to supervise its rule. Other British actions – the permitting of cow slaughter and the seizure of temple funds, for example – caused the Rani to resent the British even more. When the opportunity occurred she threw in her lot with the rebels. Of all the Indian characters in the Rebellion drama, the Rani Laksmi Bai was the most romantic and brave. She is a legend in India and is looked upon as the 'Joan of Arc' of the independence movement. Her famous reply to the British when they annexed her kingdom, 'I shall not give up my Jhansi', became a rallying cry.

In June 1857 her retainers joined the mutiny of the Company's sepoy regiments which had provided the garrison of the fort at Jhansi. The British officers and their

above: *The fort at Gwalior. Even this rocky peak and those strong, high walls and towers were scaled by a small force of British soldiers.*

left: *A statue of the Rani now stands in a beautiful public garden just below the fort at Jhansi.*

families were killed, but the Rani knew nothing of this and was not responsible for it.

For several months the British were too busy elsewhere to send forces into this area, but there was no peace. Princes and great landowners took the opportunity to revive old feuds, and in the midst of this disorder the Rani stood out as a leader of those who wanted to get rid of the British. Early in 1858 a British force under Sir Hugh Rose set about regaining control of central India. After a bloody two-day battle in the first week of April, Rose took Jhansi.

The Rani, wearing the robes of a Rajput warrior and clutching her little adopted son, escaped on horseback by leaping from the battlements of the fort down onto a hillock some way below. She joined a rebel force under Tantia Topi, who had been an officer of the Nana Sahib, and together they moved north to Kalpi.

Kalpi was an important rebel stronghold threatening Cawnpore. From here it might have been possible to revive the war in Oudh, and rebel forces from Oudh came to reinforce them. But Rose was close behind. There was a hard-fought battle, and the British won. When they took

Kalpi on 23 May the British found that the magazines contained twenty tons of gunpowder and a great quantity of weapons and ammunition. The capture of such an important arsenal was a turning point in the war.

After losing Kalpi the rebels were uncertain about their next move. The Rani of Jhansi persuaded them that they should try to make good their loss by taking another stronghold, the great fortress of Gwalior. Tantia Topi went in disguise to win over to the rebels the troops of the Maharaja of Gwalior. When the Maharaja led his little army of 2,000 to fight the rebel army of 11,000, most of his men deserted and he had to flee with his bodyguard. On 1 June the rebels moved into Gwalior and occupied the city and the fort without further opposition. They proclaimed the Nana Sahib as Peishwa and set up a government. They sent letters to the rulers of nearby states inviting them to come to Gwalior.

This was a dangerous situation for the British. They must act quickly if they were to prevent the Rebellion spreading. The Rani understood this and urged the rebel leaders to prepare Gwalior for a British counterattack, but they were

wasting time by holding parades and audiences and cele-brating their victory. Rose pushed forward at top speed, though it was the hottest time of the year, just before the rains, and many British soldiers were dying of sunstroke on the long dry marches. Rose thrust aside rebel forces in some minor battles and by 18 June he was in position in front of Gwalior. On the morning of the 19th the rebel army moved out of the city to attack him. They failed, retreated in disorder and by evening the British were dominating the city. The Rani of Jhansi, sword in hand, died in this battle. When Rose heard of it he said, 'There has passed the best and bravest leader of the rebels.'

The rebels, however, still held the fort. It is built on a great, rocky promontory nearly 2 miles (3½ km) long and 500 yards (460 metres) wide, rising 400 feet (82 metres) above the plain. The only approach is by a narrow, steep road. On the morning of 20 June two young British officers made a daring attempt on it. They took a small party of soldiers and a blacksmith and, without being seen or heard by the rebels, forced the heavy locks on a number of gates. The rest of the British forces rushed in and the fort was captured.

The recapture of Gwalior and the mopping-up operations that followed effectively ended the Rebellion in central India. Other areas were responding to an amnesty declared by the government and the great Rebellion was coming to an end. Tantia Topi, like a will-o'-the-wisp, continued to harass the British by skilful guerrilla tactics until he was betrayed to them by one of his own captains in April 1859. He was court-martialled and hanged. He died bravely, adjusting the rope round his neck with his own hands.

The end of the Rebellion

Some rebel leaders were dead and others had fled. The Nana Sahib and the Begum of Oudh took refuge in Nepal, where they died both poverty-stricken exiles. The old Emperor Bahadur Shah was tried in his own great fort at Delhi and sentenced to exile in Burma, where he died a few years later; it was a sad end to the once glorious line of Mogul Emperors.

Ordinary rebels often fared worse if they were caught alive, especially in the early months of the Rebellion. The British tried to make them fear not only death – many of

Another of the 'Cawnpore' cartoons from Punch.

THE BRITISH LION'S VENGEANCE ON THE BENGAL TIGER.

them had proved their courage in battle – but misery after death. Prisoners were blown to pieces by guns because they were thought to believe that there was no peace after death for people whose bodies were incomplete. Others were defiled and humiliated. At Cawnpore some were forced to lick clean the bloodstained walls of the place where the women and children had been butchered, though there was no proof that they were responsible.

Lord Canning, the Governor-General, saw that this sort of barbarity was useless, since it would only make the rebels more desperate, as well as being unjust. He declared that anger had no place in governing, and demanded that there be reason and justice instead of blind vengefulness. This 'softness' earned him the nickname of 'Clemency Canning' from some of the British, but eventually his orders were obeyed, and rebels were able to lay down their arms without automatically facing execution. Finally, in November 1858, the British government declared an amnesty for all rebels except those convicted of murder. At this, the time of slaughter was over.

Why had the Rebellion failed? Some of the reasons have been suggested on pages 28 and 29, and the events described in these past three chapters provide illustrations. But in the last analysis the people who win the battles win the war, and the rebels usually lost their battles even when they had far superior numbers. They were well-armed, well-trained and brave. What they lacked were commanders. None of the sepoy officers had ever commanded more than a hundred or so men. None had ever had to plan a march or a battle or a campaign, to organize large numbers and to combine infantry, cavalry and artillery. The British generals may not have been brilliant, but they did not have to learn the basic drill. Before the rebels had time to find officers able to lead them properly the Rebellion had been crushed.

Was it even one Rebellion? Perhaps the reality is that there were many mutinies and revolts which partly came together, but they were put down by British and Indian troops before they could grow into a united Rebellion. The drama involved millions, no doubt, but most of the peoples of India looked on.

9 The Indian Empire

While the Rebellion was still being put down in India, events in Britain were moving towards bringing the East India Company to an end. In Parliament it was decided that a trading company which no longer traded and which in the course of 250 years had come to rule over India as a whole (and some other parts of Asia too) was an anomaly that could only be retained if it worked well – and it had just failed disastrously. British politicians thought that such enormous power and responsibility were too much for any body less than the British government itself. Anyway, the Company had been largely under government control for a long time, and it was time to fix the responsibility where it really belonged. The British government must now face the fact that it was the ruler of the subcontinent of India, and must take its duties very seriously.

In August 1858 Queen Victoria signed the Government of India Act, whereby the government of India was assumed by the British Crown. A Secretary of State for India was appointed as a member of the British government; he was responsible to the Cabinet, and had a Council of India, composed of men with knowledge and experience of India, to advise him. The Governor-General, being now the representative of the Queen, was given the new dignity of being called Viceroy. In November came the royal proclamation which granted amnesty to the rebels. It also guaranteed freedom of religion and restored to the Indian princes the full exercise of their rights and privileges.

Obviously the most immediate task was to deal with the Indian army. It was completely reorganized as to numbers and recruiting, though it continued for the time being to be based on separate command structures for the three Presidencies. The Bengal army was started again, as from scratch. There was a policy of not recruiting men from highly orthodox religious groups, and of increasing the enlistment of Sikhs and Gurkhas. When the reorganization

The loyal Gurkhas of the 66th Regiment in their native Nepalese costume; while on duty they wore their famous rifle-green uniforms.

of the Indian army was complete in 1863 the Indian soldiers numbered 140,000 and the British 65,000. All the regiments now, of course, were in the Royal Army, and one British regiment was normally brigaded with two Indian regiments. No important garrison was left without a proportion of British troops, and these alone were given artillery and put in charge of arsenals.

Although efforts were made at reconciliation, the suspicions generated by the Rebellion and its cruelties remained under the surface for a long time. People in Britain forgot the many examples of kindness and loyalty, of poor Indians feeding and sheltering fugitives, of sepoys protecting their officers. The gulf between British and Indians widened, and for most of them there was little exchange of genuine friendship or confidence. 'East is East and West is West,

A scene typical of any traditional Indian city – in this case the bazaar at Udaipur, in what is now Rajasthan. Both this and the picture opposite are from the Illustrated London News, *1858.*

and never the twain shall meet' became a common opinion on both sides, even though the poem from which the famous quotation comes was written to show how there could be respect and honour across the gulf.

Nothing could dispose of the enormous fact that the British depended on the goodwill and support of the Indian people for their continued existence in India. They could not have defeated the rebels without thousands of Indian soldiers, hundreds of thousands of Indian cooks, water-carriers and stretcher-bearers, and millions of compliant townspeople and villagers. What had been true then was still true, and the more thoughtful British realized it. It was not enough to impose on the Indians what the British deemed to be good.

At every point in the new administration efforts were made to avoid the mistakes which had caused the revolts. Taxation was adjusted to show much greater concern about its effects on peasant farmers. At the other end of the social scale, the princes' rights included the right to adopt heirs, and even to reject in their states the sort of reforms and improvements that the British continued to develop in the territories that they ruled directly. For these improvements

A railway station near Calcutta in 1867.

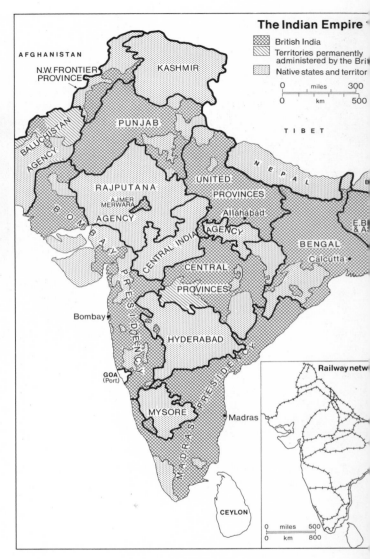

The Indian Empire

British India
Territories permanently administered by the Brit
Native states and territor

were not in themselves bad; the trouble had arisen from the way they had been introduced and thrust arrogantly on India in the years before the Rebellion.

There was a great deal of very practical work to be done. Land could be irrigated and plans made for relief in time of drought or flood. Public health could be improved by better methods of sanitation and building hospitals. Order had to be maintained so that the people could feel safe, and the courts must preserve justice and prevent corruption. All of this meant that the Viceroy's government must be able to reach all parts of the subcontinent easily, that messages, men and supplies must be able to move freely and rapidly from one part of the vast land to another. There was a great expansion of postal services, of roads and canals and, above all, railways. All these were drawing the different parts and peoples of India together into one empire. In 1876 Queen Victoria assumed the title of Empress of India. India was no longer merely part of the properties of the British Crown, but a united empire in its own right.

This adventure in empire fired the imagination of many British people at home. Working in the Indian Civil Service offered young men power and the opportunity to benefit large numbers of people, which they could not hope to attain if they stayed in Britain. The prospect was alluring, and the Indian Civil Service selected only the best; admission to the ICS was by examination, the competition was fierce and the standard very high. Some public schools specialized in preparing boys for 'leadership', to 'take up the White Man's Burden', as it was expressed by Rudyard

The proclamation of Queen Victoria as Empress of India at a great durbar in Delhi, 1877, as depicted in the Illustrated London News; a mixture of British and Indian ceremonial.

Kipling. Kipling who is often regarded as being the writer who most fully expresses the attitude of British imperialists towards the end of the nineteenth century, was born and brought up in India, and worked there as a journalist. Whatever people think of his imperialist attitude – and it is worth reading and thinking about his poems carefully before coming to any conclusion – most agree that his stories give an unrivalled and accurate picture of Queen Victoria's Indian Empire, as seen by those British who knew and loved India.

But was the view quite the same for the Indians? Did they learn to look at their world with British eyes? In the very year of the Rebellion, 1857, universities had been founded in Calcutta, Madras and Bombay. They were strongly supported, and many schools were built, both private and for the public. Here Indian children were taught what Europe had to offer, and were taught to use English. There was no other language possible, partly because the teachers used English and so did the officials, partly because to select the

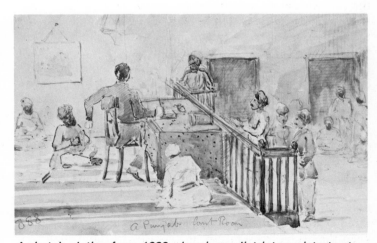

A sketch, dating from 1888, showing a district magistrate at work in a village or small town. Such men, who in practice carried most of the responsibility for the welfare of their districts, had the reputation of being able and dedicated to their work.

45

Haileybury College, a British public school which specialized in preparing boys for careers in India.

One of the buildings of the University of Bombay, thoroughly Victorian in style, with few concessions to Indian tradition.

language of any one of the many peoples of India as the all-India language would have offended the other peoples. Rich families sent their sons to schools in England, and to the universities of Oxford and Cambridge if possible. But when they had completed their education and become officials or lawyers in India, and were beginning to look forward to obtaining positions of real power, they often found that they were disappointed. When it came to entrusting Indians with authority, British feelings of superiority over 'the natives', no matter how educated and 'westernized', too often came to the surface. It was very frustrating for an Indian to be enabled and indeed encouraged to qualify himself according to British ideas, and then to be denied the jobs at which he was aiming.

This sort of progress also led to jealousy between groups of Indians. The Muslims, because Delhi and Oudh were both Muslim, found after the Rebellion that the British thought them particularly to blame. At first they tended to keep themselves resentfully to themselves, until they saw that they were throwing away possible advantages by rejecting western education. Then some of them became keen students and entered the competition for official and professional appointments. Unhappily, the advance of Mus-

lims brought them into conflict with the interests of Hindus. Rivalries increased, and widened the religious and cultural divisions which already existed.

Some orthodox religious groups, both Hindu and Muslim, continued to view the westernization of India with distaste. They took refuge by becoming more deeply immersed in their own religious beliefs and social customs. Some became more inward-looking, and revived strict observance of the teachings of their faiths. Such people undoubtedly made Indians more aware of the value of their own traditional cultures, but they also probably made the different groups less tolerant of one another. They were important, but they did not take a direct part in political life.

As time went on it was the English-speaking Indians, who had studied the political and social writings of European reformers and who had passed the examinations set in a British educational system, who began to claim the right to take upon their own shoulders the burden of ruling India.

10 Evidence and opinions

The events of the Indian Mutiny, as the British chose to call it, made a great impact not only upon British opinion at home but also upon the people of Europe and the United States.

Generally the newspapers of the western world told the harrowing story of the war in a way which was very sympathetic to the British. They extolled the extraordinary heroism of a heavily outnumbered army and the courage of the women who, at the side of the soldiers, suffered unbelievable hardships and dangers. This was true, but it was only one side of the story.

Even from the British side, a great deal was not clear. Because some of the chief incidents in the Rebellion occurred in isolated areas where perhaps only one or two British officials had the responsibility of governing many thousands of Indians, it was extremely difficult to produce a true and complete account of what had actually happened. Some of these officials had been killed, others had fled from their posts.

After the war, the British Parliament and the government of India tried to ascertain the causes of the outbreaks in various parts of northern India. Was the Rebellion a conspiracy on the part of the Muslims who had ruled most of India before the British came? Was it a war of national independence or simply a military mutiny? How much were the princes involved? Who was to blame? How should such an occurrence be prevented in future?

Partly as a result of this inquiry, various civilian officials, the survivors, wrote narratives of the happenings in their districts. Many military officers wrote their accounts of the battles and skirmishes and so did a few ordinary soldiers. An Indian official, Syed Ahmed Khan, wrote a report for the government on what he saw as the chief causes of the Rebellion. There is no shortage of personal memoirs and journalists' accounts from the winning side, but unfortunately it is very different when we look for evidence of what it looked like from the rebel side. A scribe in Delhi wrote a diary of events at the court of Bahadur Shah, which formed much of the evidence at the Emperor's subsequent trial for treason. This is the only information we have for what happened in the capital for about a year.

Of other sorts of first-hand evidence there is surprisingly little, considering that it was so huge an event and happened at a time when government officials, and others, kept voluminous records. Much of what would have been useful to historians, land and taxation documents, military ledgers and reports and so on, was destroyed in the fires of war.

For many years the British view of the Rebellion, based upon one-sided and insufficient evidence, was harshly critical of Indians. The undoubted bravery of the British was set beside exaggerated ideas of their virtues as administrators and bringers of civilization. Very little mention was made of their mistakes or of the brutality with which some of the soldiers treated Indians, innocent and guilty alike.

Not surprisingly, the views of Indian historians, some of whom were involved in the later movements for independence, were correspondingly harsh towards the British. Some could see nothing good in anything the British had done in all their time in India. They tended to see the great Rebellion simply in terms of a war for independence, and to give too little attention to the other factors and motives involved.

Deliberately or unknowingly, there were historians on both sides who were in fact using history to justify the political activities of their own people.

When the independence of India became an accomplished fact, and as the years went by, so the bitterness and recriminations died down. Historians find it easier, as a result, to do their real job of trying to understand rather than take sides. It is very difficult to be fair when there has been so much emotion and propaganda. Here, for instance, is what an Indian school history book published in 1960 has to say about events in Cawnpore:

NANA SAHIB

Nana Sahib, a friend of Tantia Tope, led the revolt against the British at Kanpur. More than four hundred Englishmen with a number of women and children defended themselves against Nana Sahib's angry men but finally had to surrender.

That is all. Not a word about the massacre. But before we condemn the author for suppressing the truth we should read on. There is not a word about the British atrocities either. Any historian has to select what he or she thinks is most important, and helps his readers to understand events clearly. There could be a great deal of honest disagreement about whether or not it is wisest to forget the evil on both sides, especially in a book meant for children.

There remain many unanswered questions about events and people in India of 1857 and 1858. Who knows how much material exists still in forgotten diaries in British homes or in dusty documents in the archives of Indian temples and mosques? How much could we learn about facts and people's attitudes from songs and stories handed down among the Indian people? It will be a long time before historians can feel that the last word has been said on what some call the Mutiny and others the great Rebellion. But, whatever else they argue about, they are all likely to agree that it was a major turning-point in the emergence of modern India.

above: *The Mourning Angel monument, erected by the British in Cawnpore; in memory of the massacred women and children. It used to stand in the middle of the city, near the well into which the bodies were thrown, but since Independence it has been moved outside the city. The marble statue was made by the sculptor Marochetti.*

right: *On the banks of the Gumti River at Lucknow, just beyond the Residency, stands this monument. It was erected by the government of India, after Independence, to those many thousands of Indian people, Hindus and Muslims, who died during the Rebellion and afterwards in the long struggle for freedom from foreign occupation and rule.*